Crstello

HAWAII

MOLOKAI
Hoolehua
Kualapuu
Mauna Loa
Kaunakakai
MAUI
Spreckelsville
Kahului
Paia
Lahaina
Puunene
Wailuku
Lanai City
LANAI
KAHOOLAWE

Honokaa
Paauilo
Papaikou
Hilo
Keaukaha
Keaau (Olaa)
Kurtistown
Pahoa
Captain Cook
Hawaii
Volcanoes
National Park
Pahala
Naalehu
HAWAII

Maui
155°

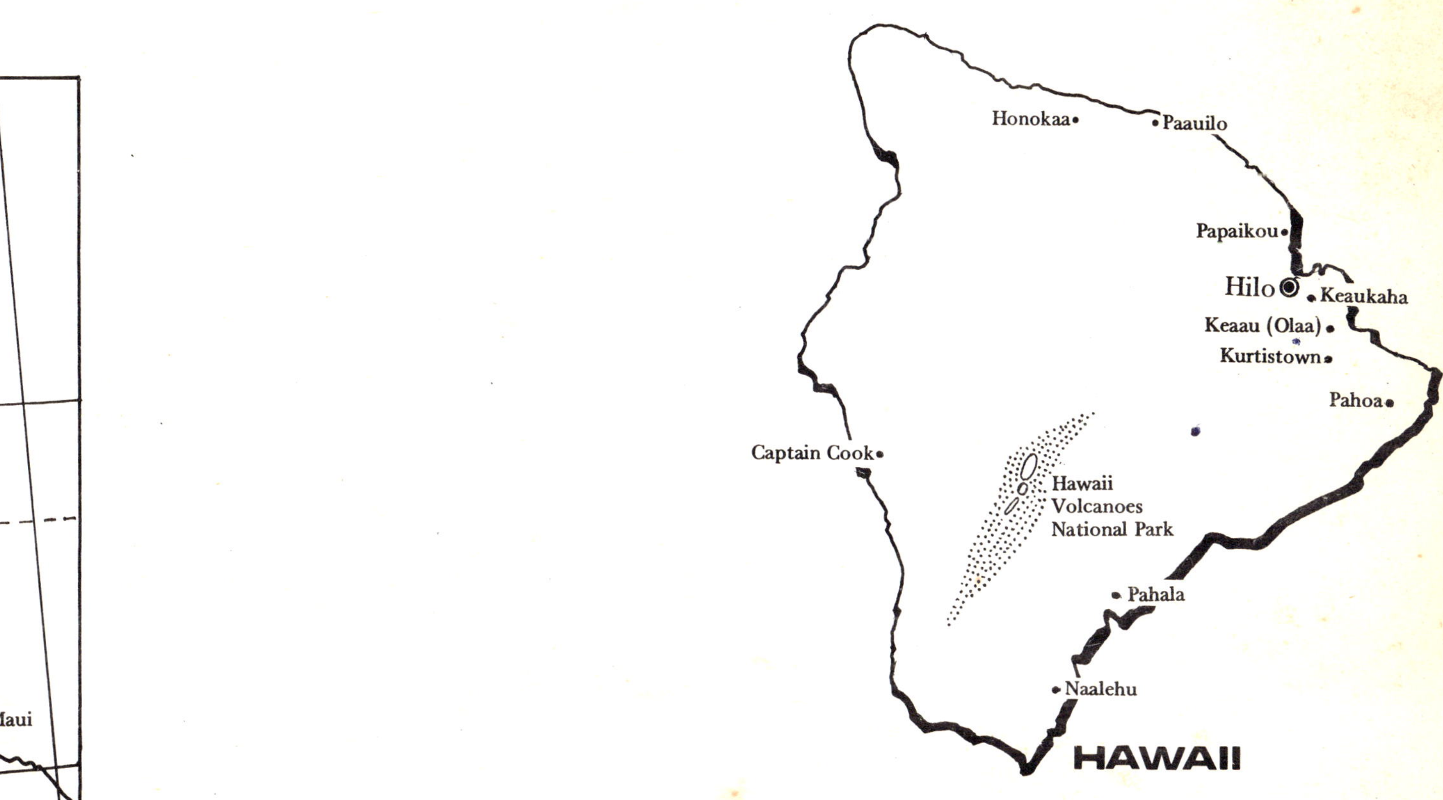

HAWAII

For information address
Harper & Row, Publishers, Inc.
10 East 53rd Street,
New York, N.Y. 10022

Produced by James Siers
Designed by Peter Redstone
Type set in New Zealand

Library of Congress Card Number: 72-11250
ISBN 06-013769-X

Printed in Taipei, Taiwan by the
China Color Printing Co., Inc.,
for Harper & Row, Publishers, Inc.

First published 1973

HAWAII

James Siers

HARPER & ROW, PUBLISHERS
New York, Evanston, San Francisco, London

1817

ACKNOWLEDGEMENTS

My sincere thanks to all those who helped me, particularly Bill and Mary Tiger, Les Enderton, Kelvin Soma, Marge Studer, Roger Ritchie, Jack Harter, Rick Printup, Roger Hawley, Randy Lee and Kristen Randall.

I would also like to thank the Avis Rent A Car System, American Airlines, Hawaiian Airlines, Inter-Island Resorts, Hawaiian Helicopters International and Sea Life Park.

Mahalo nui loa.

To maintain authenticity, the original spelling has been used when quoting from the journals from Cook's Third voyage.

INTRODUCTION

It is all true about Hawaii and more besides. The torrent of superlatives in tourist brochures is right. The unbelievable stories of those who have been there are correct; the most outlandish cliches are fact.

Hawaii, for example, is an overwhelming jumble of Polynesian, Oriental and European cultures and yet it remains peculiarly American. Part of a republic, it is inordinately proud of its past royal heritage — a former monarchy admired by the children of those who helped to pull it down.

Hawaii has Hawaiian place names, foods, songs, customs and clothes. It does not have many pure Hawaiians. This does not bother the tourist industry which lives on the legend, or the tourists who are perfectly happy to accept anything with a Hawaiian label.

Among the Hawaiians are some who have vast fortunes and others who have nothing. Some have inherited their wealth from their former chiefly families, others like Don Ho, are local boys who've made good on their own. He is one of the world's top entertainers and jokes about his Hawaiian ancestry and the various blood mixtures in his veins. As you hear him tell it, he has just about every nationality in him and sufficient Chinese as well, "in case they ever take over."

There is an air of total possibility about Hawaii. The economy booms. The sun shines. The sugar cane and the pineapples grow. The cattle are sleek on the slopes of Waimea and the tourists come each year like a wealthy drove of lemmings, to be greeted by one of the world's most impressive tourist industries. This is just another superlative in a land of superlative abundance: Hawaii has the world's biggest pineapple plantation; the biggest privately owned cattle ranch in the United States; the most efficient sugar industry; the world's most active volcanoes; it is a sub-tropical island where it is possible to ski; it has the world's highest mountain if you measure Mauna Kea from its base on the bottom of the sea . . .

And having made my way over it with a camera, I would like to confirm a superlative of my own: in its way it is the most spectacular place in the world. I hope this book proves it.

James Siers

PRE-HISTORY

Polynesian navigators discovered the Hawaiian archipelago probably before 500 A.D. — possibly much earlier. Present archaeological and linguistic evidence shows that the first settlers arrived from the Marquesas Islands about two thousand miles to the south-east. The large amount of evidence accummulated by the Anthropology Department of the Bernice P. Bishop Museum in Honolulu, also gives the Marquesas Islands a much more prominent role in the settlement of East Polynesia.

The story of Polynesian migration and settlement is elusive. Painstaking detective work in remote islands where a chance tidal wave exposes some long-forgotten village site, or the wind riffling through sand on a beach exposes the bone of a skeleton or a fish hook, has finally outlined what may have happened. Until a reliable dating method was found, all the evidence accummulated through laborious archaeological digging, was not specific. The discovery of carbon 14 as a way of measuring the age of the objects was also a way of measuring the possible settlement periods of the various island groups.

The Polynesian epic began somewhere in South East Asia. Possibly it could have begun in Indonesia where the remains of man have been found as far back as 20,000 years ago. Java is the cradle of an ancient civilisation. It could be that this was a launching point not only to the east, but also to the north, to the mainland. It is certain that when the predecessors of the Hawaiians first began moving south-east from the Indonesian-New Guinea-Philippine area that South East Asia was well-settled and culturally developed. The various ethnic groups living there spoke the same language and enjoyed the material benefits of cloth-making, agriculture, animal husbandry, fishing and navigation.

The latest theory suggests that there was no such thing as a Polynesian race in South-East Asia. It suggests instead that groups from this area of various ethnic origins, who shared its common cultural benefits, sailed in search of new lands to the south, south-east and east. Among the migrants were the oceanic Negritoid people who today occupy Papua-New Guinea, New Britain, the Solomons, Hebridies, New Caledonia, Fiji and formally Tasmania.

Carbon dating establishes the arrival of migrants in Fiji in 1500 B.C. suggesting the original dispersal from the Indonesian-Philippine islands to have occurred two or three thousand years previously. The discovery of this early occupation in Fiji and the subsequent work has resulted in a new theory on the origins of Polynesian people.

This theory, supported by archeological discoveries and language studies holds that Fiji was the cradle of the Polynesian race and culture. It suggests that various ethnic groups arrived in Fiji and lived here for a thousand years gradually evolving into a distinct race. At what point the Melanesian Negritoid peoples came in and how much they influenced the development of the Polynesian race is not certain but it seems obvious that there was considerable inter-action and that finally the Polynesians were expelled to the east to Tonga and from there to Samoa and the islands of east Polynesia.

The Marquesan Islands are identified as one of the groups which was first settled from the west. A casual look at a map of the South Pacific shows that the islands of Tahiti (Society Islands) and the Tuamotu Archipelago are much closer to Samoa than the Marquesas. It seems strange that the first voyage of discovery should have fetched up on this formidable island group, having passed so many more attractive islands on the way. It is also clear that the people of this canoe or fleet of canoes were hardly, and amply prepared to utilise their new home which was suitable to their purpose without great amendment. The taro, plantains, breadfruit, sugarcane, paper mulberry, kava root, sweet potato and coconut, which were their principal crops, thrived. The pigs, fowl and dogs multiplied. The sparse settlements spread and in no time at all, following disputes, wars and the ambitions of second sons, new canoes put out into the sea in search of other islands.

Early navigators found ample evidence of the seafaring qualities of Polynesians. The fact that they had discovered all the major island groups in the Pacific and most of the smaller ones also, was proof enough. Tupaia, the high priest from Raiatea, who joined Captain James Cook at Tahiti knew of the existence of 130 islands, but in the map he drew for Cook, he listed only 74. In that list Tupaia named Rotuma, some 500 miles to the west of the Samoan Islands; the Samoan Islands listed by their current names and in their proper order of Savai'i to the West, Upolu, Tutuila and Manu'a, the northern islands of the Tonga group, the Cook Islands, the Australs; to the east the Tuamotu atolls and (surprisingly) Mangareva and the remote Pitcairn Islands but does not list Easter Island, New Zealand and the Islands of Hawaii. To the north, the Marquesas Islands are listed with Tupaia's description: "he ma'a te ta'ata" (food is man) indicating that the islands were known to Tahitians for the ferocious cannibalism that was carried on there.

Surprisingly, the islands of Hawaii, New Zealand and Easter Island were no longer known.

Captain Cook wrestled with the origins of the Polynesians and came to the conclusion that it was perfectly possible they had come from the west. In his journal he noted: "In these pahee's as they call them from all the accounts we can learn, these people sail those seas from Island to Island for several hundred leagues, the sun serving them for a compass by day and the moon and Stars by night. When this comes to be proved we shall no longer be at a loss to know how the Islands lying in those seas came to the peopled, for if the inhabitants of Uleitea (Raiatea) having been at Islands laying 2 or 300 leagues to the westward of them it cannot be doubted but that the inhabitants of those western islands may have been at others as far to westward of them and so we may trace them from Island to Island quite to the East Indias."

A league represents three geographical miles and 300 leagues to the west of Raiatea lies the Samoan archipelago. By Tupaia's account, Tahitian voyaging pahi could sail that distance in ten to 12 days with the south-east trades behind them, but spent 30 days or more on the return leg.

The argument which began at this point of time has continued until the present. Could they navigate. Did the Polynesians have the capacity to go against the south-east and north-east trade winds. How long would their provisions last. Fortunately, a renewed interest in this question is at last beginning to turn up evidence which goes beyond the point of speculation and it is coming out increasingly in favour of the maritime ability of the people who were aptly called "The Vikings of the Sunrise."

THE FIRST HAWAIIANS

They came from the south east; the violent and cannibal islands of the Marquesas. Perhaps they were political refugees given the choice of annihalation at home or an easy exit in provisioned double canoes. A fleet of four such canoes left the Marquesas in the early 1800s, watched by a European ship. In the great continents of Europe and Asia similar movements occurred on land. What made these first migrants go to the north-west will never be understood, but as has been pointed out by Dr. Ben Finney in his essay on Polynesian migrations (Essays in Honour of Kenneth P. Emory, Bishop Museum Special Publication No 56, 1967.) the voyage would have been a relatively easy one. The canoe would have had favourable north-east trades when past the equator and these would be at an angle suited to the craft.

Perhaps some day archaeology will unearth a clue as to where those settlers landed and established their first settlement. It is certain that they must have been delighted with their large and uninhabited home in every way suited to their way of life; from the climate to the reassuring similarity with the ruggedness of the geographical features. Much like the Marquesas, the Hawaiian chain of islands which stretches over 1500 miles of ocean, covering nearly 6500 square miles with land, is exposed on one side to the trade winds. These drop their moisture and drape the windward side of the islands with a rich, verdant tropical rain forest and a climate perfectly suited to the cultivation of the main food crops brought in the migration. Some of the islands, such as Kauai, (aptly called the garden isle) get a more even distribution of rainfall. The settlement of the Hawaiian chain would have followed a pattern similar to the one already established by the ancestors of Polynesians in countless other migrations. The first village with the stone alter to thank the gods of the ocean for a safe voyage; offerings to Rongo (subsequently the Hawaiian god Lono) the god of agriculture for a safe acclimatisation of plants; the dispersal of family groups into new fertile valleys and the steady build up of the population. The principal islands of the group are visible next to each other on clear days from a high point. There would have been little difficulty in crossing from one to the other and having done so, in maintaining communication. Perhaps the first settlers came in a fleet of canoes, in which case the colonisation would have been much more rapid. Before long the fertile parts of the islands were planted out in groves of coconut, taro, breadfruit, sugar cane, banana, sweet potato, paper mulberry for the production of *tapa* cloth; *kava* root cultivated for use in ceremonial occasions. The animals brought in the canoes would also find Hawaii a provident home. Pigs, dogs and jungle cock acclimatised easily to their new environment.

It is not certain at what point the first Tahitians arrived in the Hawaiian islands. Oral tradition spoke of Kahiki (Tahiti) as the home of the Hawaiians. Scientists waited for more ample evidence. In 1962 a Tahitian turned up in his garden in Raiatea a small stone disk. It was flat on one side, convex on the other and had a notch on its edge. Bishop Museum scientists identified this as a game stone found only in Hawaii and Tahiti, no longer in use at the time of European contact. Additional evidence in the form of fish-hooks similar in both Hawaii and Tahiti, suggests, says Dr. Emory, the dean of Polynesian research, that two-way voyaging was a feature between the two archipelagos. When the first contact was established and at what point it ended, is not known.

Hawaiian legend suggests that the Tahitian incursion into the Hawaiian islands had a considerable cultural impact. There is the story of the high priest Paao, who built the *heiau* at Wahaula, not far from the famous black sand beach at Kalapana in the Volcanoes National Park on the big island of Hawaii. It is said that he found the power of the chiefs and priests of the first Hawaiians considerably lapsed, and he knew exactly how to restore it. Paao introduced a system of strict *tapus* (kapus) and to enforce these, human sacrifice to the gods. As in Tahiti a man who had broken a *kapu* or who was troublesome to his chiefs, was a proper offering to the gods. Part of the *heiau* remains at Wahaula, apt testimony to the consolidation of power by the aristocracy through the help of a priestly caste. The classic period of Hawaiian culture had arrived.

At this time the islands, as in Tahiti, were divided into a number of political states ruled by paramount chiefs. They were aided and supported by lesser land-holding chiefs who made sure that the commoners met their production quotas of food and other goods which were part of the material culture. There were priodic wars but there was no premanent state of war as in the Marquesas and there is no record of cannibalism. The crops flourished and the tedium of hard work was broken with religious observances, chiefly celebrations and festivals. The Hawaiian loved to sing, to dance and to make love; his ambition was aided by the climate and the beauty of the surroundings.

EUROPEAN DISCOVERY

It was at this point that the famous English navigator and explorer, Captain James Cook, chanced upon their islands. It was an inevitable discovery in an age of tremendous European naval exploration and just as inevitably it was to lead to tragedy for the Hawaiian. In 1776 when Cook impetuously agreed to his third voyage of exploration at a dinner with his patron and friend Lord Sandwich, he was already at the height of his renown. A steady Yorkshireman with a bulldog tenacity, he had earned the respect of the Lords of the Admiralty, his fellow officers and the "people" — the hard, lusty mutinous English sailors. Cook was marked for promotion because of his work in the St. Lawrence River in the war against the French. His first voyage into the Pacific in 1768-71 recognised his merit as a navigator, cartographer and humanitarian. The first voyage was scientific. It was to observe the transit of the planet Venus across the disc of the sun as an aid to navigation. Admiralty ships were to be sent to Hudson Bay and to Scandinavia for the same purpose. Cook was to proceed to Tahiti, discovered in the previous year by another Englishman, Captain Wallis of H.M.S. *Dolphin.* Cook was also instructed to take on board the *Endeavour* a gentleman botanist, Mr Joseph Banks and the scientists and artists in his party. It was a brilliant party whose intense, objective scientific work lives on to this day. The voyage was successful. Cook arrived in Tahiti, made his observations and went on to raise new islands in the course of his circumnavigation.

In 1772-75 he made another voyage. This time with two ships, the Resolution and Adventure. It was to establish if the theory of a great southern continent was correct. It was popularly believed that there must be a great land mass in the lower southern latitudes to "balance" continental Europe and Asia. Otherwise, the argument went, the world would tip over. Cook had already established during his previous voyage that New Zealand, discovered by Abel Tasman during his voyage of 1642-43, was an island and not part of such a continent. He would use it, however, as a base for a careful search that would take him into the ice of Antarctica, where he would find his continent, but one which would not be of use economically or strategically at that time.

His third and final voyage in 1776-1780 was to end in personal tragedy for Cook. He was killed by the Hawaiians at Kealakekua Bay on the Island of Hawaii in February 1779 during a misunderstanding. This voyage, like the previous one, was also to establish a theory. It was an exciting theory, full of economic and political implications — that a passage existed between the north Atlantic and the north Pacific which would offer a quick passage from

Britain for trade with Cathay or to naval ships in times of dispute with France or Spain. It was a theory tested in the cold waters of Hudson's and Baffin's Bays by the British with the loss of lives. Some fifty voyages had already been made in quest of this passage and those that came back varied in their opinions. Always possibilities remained to be tried again, ever spurred by the fact that Magellan had found the south-west passage round the Horn into the Pacific and that sooner or later someone would find the north-west passage round the tip of North America. The theorists were right. There is a passage but it isn't navigable to ordinary ships. It took the great oil discovery in Alaska and the subsequent problem of the transportation of the oil, before it was discussed again. Vast ships with icebreaking capacity were talked of. In the days of Cook they were small ships made of wood, rigged with canvas and provisioned with salt beef and pork.

Cook's mission was to look for the passage from the Pacific side. If in fact the continents of Asia and America were separated by a passage as Russian explorations suggested, then there was the possibility of a north-east passage. Cook was to look for both. On board the *Resolution* was William Bligh, at 22 years her master, a responsible position. He was to figure in several dramatic incidents in the Pacific and to survive three mutinies. His first mutiny on H.M.S. Bounty near Tonga, in April 1789, was the most famous. Bligh was put off in the ship's launch and sailed more than three thousand five hundred miles to Java with the loss of only one man. During Cook's third voyage he earned favourable mention for his excellent surveying and charting. Another man who was to figure prominently later was George Vancouver.

Cook sailed from Porstmouth in the *Resolution* on July 12, 1776. Captain Charles Clerke was to follow him in the *Discovery*. Both ships were to rendezvous at the Cape of Good Hope, but Clerke arrived nearly a month later. The ships were overhauled, provisioned and left the Cape on the 1st of December on a south-east course round the bottom of Tasmania, calling into Adventure Bay to gather grass for the stock on board the *Resolution,* a gift from the British Monarch to the people of Tahiti, and to cut spars. Ten days later he was in New Zealand in his favourite anchorage in Queen Charlotte Sound. It was here on his previous voyage that he lost five men to the cannibal Maoris. He was to meet the man who had been the principal in the plot and to show himself humanitarian in not taking revenge. Other naval captains had less reserve.

On February, 25th the ships left New Zealand for Tahiti, met contrary winds and a month later were still six hundred miles off from their destination. Cook lost patience and changed course for Tonga, calling in desperation at Palmerston Atoll in the Cook group to get fodder for the starving stock. In this region he also raised a number of new islands of the Southern Cooks — the only islands in the vast region to be explored and raised by him that bear his name. The ships spent 11 weeks in Tonga unaware that the Tongans had planned to massacre the crews. The plan failed because there was no agreement among the principal chiefs as to the best means of attack. Cook called the Tongan group the "Friendly" Islands.

The epic voyage continued. In August the ships were at Tahiti. They landed their cargo of livestock and Omai, the Tahitian who had lived for several years in England, having been brought back, among other curiosities in Cook's earlier voyage. In November they are on the way to "New Albion" on the northern coast of America. On December the 24th, his second Christmas at sea, he raised an island and named it Christmas Island. It was uninhabited but had ample evidence of the presence of earlier Polynesian navigators. The ships were underway again on the 2nd of January and on the 18th, sighted land. The Hawaiian chain, the last great stronghold of the Polynesians, was pencilled into a European chart. The first island raised was Oahu, then Kauai and finally Niihau. Contrary winds prevented a landing at Oahu.

On Monday the 19th of January as Cook pulled in towards land off Kauai he wrote in his journal: "At this time we were in some doubt whether or not the land before us was inhabited, this doubt was soon cleared up, by seeing some canoes coming off from the shore towards the ships, I immediately brought to to give them time to come up, there were three and four men in each one, we were agreeably surprised to find them of the same Nation as the people of Otahiete and the other islands we had lately visited. It required but little address to get them to come alongside but we could not prevail upon anyone to come on board; they exchanged a few fish they had in the Canoes for anything we offered them, but valued nails, or iron above every other thing; the only weapons they had were a few stones in some of the canoes and these they threw overboard when they found they were not wanted. Seeing no signs of an anchoring place at this part of the island, I boar up for the lee side, and ranged the SE (south-east) side at the distance of half a league from the shore. As soon as we made sail the canoes left us, but others came off from the shore and brought with them roasting pigs and some very fine potatoes (sweet potatoes), which they exchanged, as the others had done, for whatever was offered them; several small pigs were got for a sixpenny nail (so called because they cost 6 pence per 100) or two apiece, so that we again found ourselves in the land of plenty, just as the turtle we had taken on board at the last island was nearly expended. We passed several villages, some seated upon the sea shore and others up in the Country; the inhabitants of all of them crowded to the shore and on the elevated places to view the Ships. The land on this side of the island rises in a gentle slope from the sea shore to the foot of the Mountains that are in the middle of the island, except in one place, near the east end where they rise directly from the sea; here they seemed to be formed of nothing but stone which lay in horizontal stratas; we saw no wood but what was up in the interior part of the island and a few trees about the villages; we observed several plantations of Plantains and sugar canes, and places that seemed to be planted with roots . . . "

Sounding carefully over the uncertain bottom the ships were be-nighted and spent the night standing off and on. Cook's journal continues: "The next morning we stood in for the land and were met by several Canoes filled with people, some of them took courage and ventured on board. I never saw Indians so much astonished at the entering of a ship before, their eyes were continually flying from object to object, the wildness of their looks and actions fully expressed their surprise and astonishment at the several new objects before them and evinced that they never had been on board of a ship before."

This is a significant point as the argument still rages that the Spaniard Gaetano had discovered the group previously. One of the officers, James King remarks in his journal: "We took some of them into the Gunroom to observe their behaviour and to put Questions to them; when we asked them what this Iron was, and where it came from, they told us, they did not know but that we knew; when we shewd them beads they asked if they shou'd eat them, or what was their use, we told them only to hang to their Ears, on which they returned them to us as useless, for their ears are not pierced; they also returnd looking Glasses, saying they did not know what these things were for; and of Iron they only knew its use for boring and to make Toes (Hatchets) and wantd them large."

The mutual examination continued with interest. The Englishmen by now — some of them having been to Tahiti three times, as well as at various other Polynesian Islands — knew how to speak sufficient Polynesian to talk to the Hawaiians. It seems also, from the journal that in Kauai in particular at that time, "t" was still being used instead of "k" as in Tahiti. The island was known as Tauai. "R" was used in place of "l", as in Tahiti.

The ships came in close to the shore and a boat was sent to look for fresh water. A Hawaiian tried to take the sounding lead and line, but was persuaded to give it up. But another got hold of the butcher's cleaver, leapt overboard, made his canoe and outstripped the boats which pursued him.

Cook was now planning to go ashore at the first opportunity but he was concerned about the medical condition of some of his men: "As there were some veneral complaints on board both the Ships, in order to prevent its being communicated to these people, I gave orders that no Women, on any account whatever were to be admitted on board the Ships, I also forbid all manner of connection with them, and ordered that none who had the veneral upon them should go out of the ships."

The regulations, unfortunately, did not have the desired effect.

By now the ships were standing on and off the coast near Waimea. The boat sent ashore to look for water returned. Lt. Williamson, who was in charge, reported that he had pulled into shore near a village but that the Hawaiians had come down in great numbers and prevented his landing. A man had laid hold of his gun and Williamson shot him dead. There was considerable speculation as to whether this was a threatening gesture. Those in the boat felt that the Hawaiian was only trying to help the boat land through the surf as were others who took hold of the oars and sides of the boat.

Cook sent one of the boats to find a good anchoring ground and then moved in and anchored in 25 fathoms of water opposite what is now the township of Waimea. As soon as the ships were fast, Cook went ashore "to look at the water and try the disposition of the inhabitants, several hundred of whom were assembled on a sandy beach before the village. The very instant I leaped ashore, they all fell flat on their faces, and remained in that humble posture till I made signs to them to rise." Cook was taken for the highest rank of chief and treated as such by the Hawaiians.

There followed presentations of food and professions of friendship which Cook reciprocated. A stone with a brass plaque now marks the spot at the mouth of the Waimea river. On the opposite side on the raised ground lays the ruin of a Russian fort and the township of Waimea is a quaint village with a mid-Western facade. There is little to suggest that first meeting.

The English remained at their anchoring place for three days. Cook and some of the officers not involved in watering and trading were taken on conducted tours around the countryside; they visited *heiaus* which they found very much like those of Tahiti; *taro* patches; banana groves; sugar cane; paper mulberry trees; coconut trees but saw only one breadfruit tree.

On Thursday the 22nd of January Cook moved the *Resolution* because of a change of wind which caused a heavy surf to break a short distance from the ship. Despite several attempts to regain his former anchoring place he was unable to do so. A landing was made on the 30th at Niihau. The next day Cook landed and presented to the people three goats: a buck and two nannies; a boar and sow; the seeds of mellon, pumpkin and onion. The English conducted some more trade and with the weather deteriorating again, he stood off, signalled the *Discovery* to join him, and made for the coast of North America.

As the ships got underway Cook, Clerke and the other officers and some of the men who kept journals, found time to make observations about this first meeting with the Hawaiians. Cook wrote:

"I have already observed that these people are of the same nation as the people of Tahiti and many others of the South Sea islands, consequently they differ but little from them in their persons. These have a darker hue than the generality of the Tahitians, which may be owing to their being more exposed to the Sun and wearing less clothing. How shall we account for this Nation spreading it self so far over this Vast ocean? We find them from New Zealand to the South, to these island to the North and from Easter Island to the Hebridies; an extent of 60 degrees of latitude or twelve hundred leagues north and south and 83 degrees of longtitude or sixteen hundred and sixty leagues east and west, how much farther is not known, but we may safly conclude that they extend to the west beyond the Hebridics.

"These people are scanty in their clothing, very few of the Men wear anything more than the Maro, but the women have a piece of cloth wraped around the waist, so as to hang down like a petticoat as low as the knee; all the rest of the body is naked. Their ornaments are bracelets, necklaces and Amulets, which are made of shells, bone or stone; They have also neat Tippets made of red and yellow feathers, and Caps and Cloaks covered with the same or some other feathers; the cloakes, reach to about the middle of the back, and are like the short cloakes worn by the women in England, or like the riding cloakes worn in Spain. The Caps are made so as to fit very close to the helmets of old. These and also cloaks they set so high a Value upon that I can not procure one, some were however got." (These were the beautiful feather cloaks and caps of chiefs and were very valuable).

"Tattowing or staining of the skin is practised here, but not in a high degree, nor does it appear to be directed to any particular mode but rather by fancy. The figures were straight lines, Stars & ca and many had the figure of the *Taame (tamai;* a fan design) or breast plate of Tahiti, though we saw it not among them. The hair is in general black were they not to stain it, as at the Friendly islands; it is worn in different forms, some have it long and some short, and some both; but the general fashion, among the women in particular, is to have it long before and short behind. Some of the men had a kind of wig made of human hair twisted together into a number of long tails, each a finger thick that hung down as low as the breach. Some of the men had long beards but the general custom was to have it short. They are an open, candid, active people and the most expert swimmers we had met with; in which they are taught from their very birth: It was very common for women with infants at the breast to come off in Canoes to look at the Ships, and when the surf was so high that they could not land them in the Canoe they used to leap over board with the child in their arms and make their way to shore through surf that looked dreadfull. It hath been mention that I did not see a chief of note, there were however several on Atoui (Kauai) and one of them called Tamahano, made Captain Clerke a visit after I had left the island. He came off in a double canoe, and like the King of the Friendly islands, paid no regard to those who happened to lay in his way but ran against or over them without endeavouring in the least to avoid them; nor could they get out of his way as the people in them were obliged to lay down till he had passed. His attendents helped him into the Ship and placed him on the gangway, and were so carefull of him that they stood around him with their hands locked with each other, not suffering any one to come near him but Captain Clerke. He was a young man, cloathed from head to foot and accompanied by a young woman, suppos'd to be his wife. Captain Clerke made him some suitable presents and in return he gave him a large Cava bowl, that was supported by two carved men, neither ill designed nor executed. Cava or Ava-Ava as it is called at Tahiti is prepared and drank here as at the other islands. Captain Clerke could not prevail upon him to go below, nor move from the place he was fixed in; at length after a short stay he was conducted to shore in the same manner as he came on board. The next day several messages came off to Captain Clerke, desiring him to go ashore, and aquainting him that the Chief had a large present for him; but being anxious to get to sea he did not go.

"We had good reason to think that all the islands are subject or belong to the great men of Atoui (Kauai)."

This, however, was not so. The islands named for Cook by the people of Kauai comprised only part of the Hawaiian chain. He was to learn later that all the islands were divided into four principal kingdoms based at Kauai, Oahu, Maui and the large island of Hawaii.

Cook goes on to comment on the weapons, canoes, houses and household utensils of the Hawaiians. The weapons were spears, daggers of about a foot or more long made of wood and iron, and clubs. The canoes were both of the outrigger and double canoe type and these, he says: "are shaped and fitted with more judgement than any I had before seen." He comments also on the cloth: "But what they most excell in colouring is cloth, which, like the cloth of the other islands, is made of bark, none of it remarkably fine but it is all glazed and prented with different colours, which are so disposed as to have a pritty and pleasing effect; they have a very great variety of patterns and many of them are extremely beautiful."

Cook goes on to discuss the possession of iron by the Hawaiians; "The only iron tools or indeed pieces of iron seen among them, which they were supposed to have before our arrival, was a piece of iron hoop about three inches long, fited into a wooden handle in the same manner as their stone adzes and a nother edge tool which was supposed to have been made of the point of a broad sword. This, and their knowing the use of iron made some imagine that we were not the first Ships that had been at these islands, on the other hand the very great surprise they shewed at the sight of the ships and their total ignorance of fire arms seemed to prove the contrary. There are many ways by which these islands as well as many others, may come by the knowledge of iron without being visited by shipping; for without mention the intercourse which one group may have with another, is there not the whole coast of America to windward, where the Spaniards have been settled for more than two hundred years and where Shipwrecks must have frequently happened. It therefore cannot be thought an extrordenary thing for part of such wrecks with iron in it, to be now and then cast upon islands, scatered about this vast ocean; the distance is no argument whatever against it; but even if it was, it would not distroy it, as many things containing iron may be thrown out, or lost from ships that have made passage across this ocean, such as the loss of a mast and many other things which must be obvious to every one. But what confirms it is one of my people seeing some wood in one of the houses at Waimea, which he judged to be fir; it had been eat by the worm and the people made him to understand that it was driven a shore by the waves of the sea."

The ships were now well on their way to the "frozen secrets of the Artic," as Capt Clerke, of the *Discovery,* put it. The ships left the Hawaiian waters in February, it was not until the end of November, that they were to return again.

DEATH OF JAMES COOK

On October the 26th, 1778, the ships returned to Hawaii. The land first seen was Maui, the second largest island of the group. At noon the ships were off Kahului and brought to, to allow canoes which were seen leaving the land to come up. Among those that came on board were some who had been at Kauai when the ships had called there. Cook also comments that his strict instructions that men with veneral disease should not communicate with women had failed during his previous call: " . . . it appears rather too evident as these people had got amongst them the Veneral distemper, and I as yet know of no other way they could come by it."

Entries in other journals say the same; that it was a new disease brought to the other islands from Kauai, following the previous visit of the English ships.

Trade was resumed, but Cook would not allow his people ashore. The women who came off in canoes to the ship, were turned away, for which, comments one of the midshipmen: "They abused us most sincerely."

The ship now tacked to the north-east and on the afternoon of the 30th of December off Hana was met by a fleet of canoes and a chief of high standing: Kalaniopuu, the principal chief or "king" of the Island of Hawaii. He was accompanied by his courtiers and among them a young man named Kamehameha, who chose to remain on board for the night. As the ships rounded the north-east point they sighted the island of Hawaii to the east. Next morning when the Hawaiians learned that the ships were to continue to examine the new island, they left the ship. A footnote in the Journal of James Cook for the third voyage, edited by J.C. Beaglehole, says that Kalaniopuu was at war with Kahekili of Maui and it is obvious that Kamehameha and the others were part of an invasion force.

Slowly the ships moved round the island, trading as they went. Christmas Day was celebrated — the third at sea. Also the New Year: "Before day break the Atmosphere was again loaded with heavy Clouds, the new year was ushered in with very hard rain, which continued at intervals till past 10 o'clock . . . "

On the 16th of January the ships were off Kealakekua Bay and Bligh was sent with a boat from each ship to examine it. Canoes came off in great numbers so that before ten o'clock in the morning there were "not less than a thousand about the two ships . . . " Next day Bligh returned and said that he had found the bay suitable for anchorage and that there was fresh water available and that it was "tolerable easy to come at." During the night many of those who had come off in canoes asked to sleep on board and were allowed to do so. Cook learned the next morning that the scrupulous honesty the ships had experienced so far, was not general as some things were missing. He determined never to allow a large number to sleep on board again. As the ships came in to their anchorage they were once more crowded by a multitude of canoes and there were hundreds of others on shore, some of who swam out to the ships and were "swimming about the Ships like shoals of fish." Some were armed with tools to draw out nails which held the copper sheathing to the ship's sides and avoided the small shot being fired at them by diving under the bottom.

The English had stumbled on one of the greatest of Hawaiian festivals: the season of *Makahiki* when war was forbidden and love was the theme; when people came together for sporting competitions and hard work was forgotten. It was the time of the god *Lono;* the gentle god of ample harvests; the god whose return was expected by the Hawaiians. There is some dispute now whether Cook was accepted as the returning god. As Cook had stopped keeping his journal at this point, it is impossible to know what he thought about the ceremony which his officer James King describes:

After dinner, at which Cook had entertained the head priest, Koa and another chief, he accompanied them ashore. In the party were King himself and another officer, Bailey. They landed on the beach and were met by three or four men who held wands tipped with dog's hair, and who kept repeating a sentence using the word *Lono.* By this time Cook had already been distinguished by this name. The party moved to the *heiau* and as he looked about him King saw all the people on their hands and knees with their heads bowed towards the ground. The party went up the *heiau* which was about eight feet high from the ground but on the opposite side, where the ground fell away, it was twice that high. The top of the *heiau* was paved with stones and was surrounded with a railing, on which were stuck 20 skulls taken from Maui during recent battles. At the end were two houses and on the opposite end, a scaffolding. As the party entered the area near the houses they were stopped and Cook was presented to the carved representations of gods. The party was then led to the opposite end where the scaffold was. At the foot of the scaffolding were 12 more images ranged in a semi-circular form and opposite the central figure, on a raised platform was a pig which had been previously offered and which at this time was putrified. There was also a large offering of other food. Koa, the head priest, led Cook under the platform supporting the rotten pig and handled the pig while repeating prayers and incantations. He then took Cook to the scaffolding which both ascended. At the same time a procession of ten men approached the *heiau* and lay down on the ground. One of the priests took their offering which comprised a pig and red cloth and gave it to Koa. The high priest wrapped the cloth round Cook. The pig was then handed up and Koa repeated prayers before letting it fall. He then led Cook before the images adressing them as he went, until he came to the image in the centre before which he prostrated himself and afterwards kissed and asked Cook to do the same. Cook did everything asked of him. This we now know was the image of *Ku,* who like *Lono,* was one of the four principal Polynesian gods. The Captain was brought down following this ceremony and then after numerous presentations of food which was laid out, one of the chiefs approached chanting a litany starting with long sentences ending with the word *Lono,* and gradually shortening until the huge crowd about the *heiau* was repeating only the word *Lono.* It would seem fair to suppose that Cook, considered the god *Lono* returned, was now diefied. Later when the feast started, Cook, mindful that the food was handed to him by Koa who had handled the rotten pig, could not eat. As King says: " . . . could not get a Morsel down, not even when the old fellow very Polietely chew'd it for him."

Life became grand for the English, despite the minor irritations of petty theft. On the 25th of January the "king" of the island, Kalaniopuu, having returned from Maui, visited the ships. The next morning he called on the *Resolution.* It must have been a beautiful scene. The large double canoes coming off; the chiefs in their scarlet feather caps and cloaks; the priests in one canoe laden with images and food, singing as they came towards the ship. As the canoes touched the ship, they turned and went back towards shore. Cook understood that this was an invitation for him and followed them. When he got ashore, Kalaniopuu "threw in a graceful manner over the Captains shoulders the Cloak he himself wore and put a feathered Cap upon his head, and a very handsome fly flap (whisk) in his hand; besides which he laid down at the Captains feet 5 or 6 Cloaks more, all very beautiful, and to them of the greatest Value; his attendants brought 4 large hogs, with other refreshments which were also presented," writes James King in his journal.

Among the retinue of chiefs, King noticed one in particular, Kamehameha. He describes him: "Amongst these was Kamehameha, whose hair was now Paisted over with a brown dirty sort of Paste or Powder, and which added to as savage a looking face as I ever saw, it however by no means seemd an amblem of his disposition which was good naturd and humorous; Although his manners shew'd somewhat of an overbearing spirit and he seem'd to be the Principal director in this interview . . . "

The thieving increased and both ships were obliged to take extra precautions. Meantime the *Resolution's* rudder had to be repaired and as much of the gear overhauled as was necessary on both ships. By the 2nd of February the chiefs were asking when the ships would leave and were pleased when told that it would be soon. The previous day William Watman, a Marine, had died and the chiefs asked that he might be buried on the *heiau* Hikiau, which stands in good repair to this day. A plaque describes the burial.

On February the 4th, the ships weighed anochor and moved out of the bay accompanied by a number of canoes. On the 7th the weather worsened and turned rough. A gale began to blow. The ship saved some people in canoes and had on board many women, abandoned by their men because of the bad weather. Next day the gales continued and Cook found the head of the foremast badly sprung. There was other damage which made it absolutely necessary to effect repairs. James King in his journal expresses the doubts of Cook and others about returning to Kealakekua Bay; they may have felt that they had outstayed their welcome. The decision was made to return and King writes: "all hands much chagrin'd and damning the Foremast."

On February 11th the ships were once more anchored in the Bay. On the 13th the foremast was taken out and taken ashore to be repaired. Although trade was resumed, there was a change of attitude among the people. The watering party was hindered by a chief who told the Hawaiians not to help with the casks despite the fact that they had been paid. A marine was posted with side arms only and the Hawaiians began to arm with stones. Another marine was sent, this time with a musket and the mob threw away its stones. The chiefs dispersed the mob and when Captain Cook came ashore he ordered that if the Hawaiians began to throw stones or were to act insolently, that a musket with a ball should be fired at them. The sentries, who until this time had their pieces loaded with shot, reloaded with ball.

While the Captain was ashore inspecting the work of repair to the mast, he heard a shooting from the *Discovery* and saw that the musket fire was directed at a canoe making away from the ship with haste. The fatal sequence of events was now in progress. James King writes in his journal:

"The Captain call'd to me to go along with him, and we took with us a Marine with his Musket and a Corporal; Our intentions were to meet the Canoe, if we could, as she came on shore, and as we had no doubt but the fyring was in Consequence of some theft, we hoped to recover the things. I outran the Captain and Soldiers, but the Canoe had reached the Shore long before I got the proper length. I was however near enough to call to Mr. Vancover (a young Gentleman of the Discovery) who pointed towards the

Shore, but the immense croud and noise of the People was such that I could not hear what he said. The Captain instead of coming towards me or nearer the Discoverys boat, kept walking on at a great rate along shore; this made me give over all thought of getting nearer Mr. Vancover in order to hear what was the matter, as I must then have lost the Captain, for it was with great difficulty I could at all join them; on coming up to him I asked him if he had heard any tidings of the thief or thing stolen, he said no, but that they point'd a little farther. We kept running on till dark and I believe more than three miles from the tent, sometimes stopping and enquiring after the thief, the Captain threatning to make the Centry fire, if they did not bring the man. Whenever the Marine made any motion of presenting, the Croud would recoil back, but it was observable enough that they began to laugh at our threat; we also remark'd that he they call'd Lono, receivd some intelligence which two or three times made the whole body fly to some distance, and we remarked large bodies collecting in all parts; it was now too late to go farther and the Captain thought it best to return, but I believe it was not from the smallest Idea of any danger. They conducted us back a very different rout, which was farther from the sea, and which as we afterwards judgd was designedly done. When we got to the tent the Captain's Coxswain acquainted him, that he, on seeing us run along, and the small boat of the Discovery's in pursuit of a Canoe went to assit, that a fray happend, in which Palea was the principal actor, by which they all got thrasht, the pinnace's oars broke all except one, and the piece of another which was all they now had. The Captain was exceeding angry at the folly of his Coxswain going to assist others, having no arms in the boat."

On board King heard more of the story. Already Cook expressed the fear that the behaviour of the Hawaiians would oblige him to use force. All the women on board were turned out. And the Discovery's master, a Mr. Edgar was asked to account for the affair. Edgar and Vancouver said that a pair of armourer's tongs and the lid of a cask had been taken from the *Discovery*. As the canoe reached shore the goods were passed to another canoe and returned to the pursuing boat. They were now satisfied and were on their way back to the ship but on seeing the pinnace (small boat with oars and sails belonging to a man-o-war) coming towards them and Captain Cook and his party running on the shore, they turned and went back to get the canoe belonging to the thieves, as well as the thieves and to take them on board.

A classic misunderstanding occurred. Palea, the chief who had been on board the *Discovery* at the time of the theft, and who was responsible for the stolen goods being returned, was now on shore. It was his canoe that the Englishmen seized. Vancouver was about to paddle it to the ship when the young chief pulled the canoe to the rocks and took the paddle. Edgar tried to get it back and the powerful Hawaiian "seiz'd on Edgar, and held him in such a manner that he could not stir," but let him go when he saw assistance coming and ran towards the pinnace. Someone in the pinnace hit him on the head with an oar and when this happened there was a tremendous shower of stones from the shore. The men in the pinnace jumped overboard and swam to a rock. The Hawaiians took the pinnace and everything in her, knocked Vancouver down and were going to strip him and were trying to knock the rings and bolts out of the pinnace when Palea stopped them. He complained of having been hit on the head and then got in his boat and went over to the village on the north side of the bay where the principal chief, Kalaniopuu, was in residence. He asked if he could come on board the following morning and was told he could.

The next day Captain Clerke of the *Discovery* was told that the large cutter, which was moored to a bouy and sunk, to prevent the sun splitting the boards, had been stolen. He went to the Resolution and informed Cook. Cook told him to take his boats to the south-east point of the bay, while he (Cook) would go to the north-west and that they were to seize all the canoes and hold them until the cutter was returned. As Clerke prepared for his part, he was told that Cook had gone ashore to the village where Kalaniopuu lived. Clerke assumed matters would soon be settled. Soon after he heard firing from the shore and saw through his telescope the landing party driven off.

Soon after he received a report from Lt Phillips, who was in charge of the Marines in the affray. Cook's party landed in the pinnace, leaving the small cutter off the point to prevent the escape of any canoes. On landing Cook ordered the detachment of Marines, comprising the officer and nine men, to march into the village with him. He was directed to the house where Kalaniopuu was still asleep. The chief's two sons led the party. The chief woke and when told that Cook was outside, came out. Cook asked the old chief to accompany him on board, intending to use him as hostage for the return of the cutter. The chief was happy to do so and the party was moving towards the boats when it was interrupted at the water's edge by one of Kalaniopuu's wives who with tears streaming down her face asked the chief not to go on board. At the same time two chiefs laid hold of him and made him sit down. The old man became frightened. The situation became tense. The party was surrounded by a huge mob of nearly three thousand people. Phillips reports that he told Cook that the Marines, who were huddled together in the midst of the throng, might be better arranged along the rocks by the water and the Captain agreed. Cook now gave up thoughts of taking the chief and said to Phillips: "we can never think of compelling him to go on board without killing a number of these people," and Phillips adds: "I believe was just going to give orders to embark, when he was interrupted by a fellow arm'd with a long iron spike which they call *pahoa* and a stone; this man made a flourish with the *pahoa,* and threatened to throw the stone upon which Captain Cook discharg'd a load of small shot at him but he having his Mat on, the small shot did not penetrate it, and had no other effect than farther to provoke and encourage them, I could not observe the least fright it occasion'd; immediately upon this an *Ali'i* arm'd with a *pahoa* attempted to stab me but I foil'd his attempt by giving him a severe blow with the Butt End of my musket, just at this time they began to throw stones, and one of the Marines was knock'd down, the Captain then fir'd a ball and kill'd a Man. They now made a general attack and the Captain gave orders to the Marines to fire and afterwards called out "Take to the Boats". I fir'd just after the Captain and loaded again whilst the Marines fir'd; almost instantaneously upon my repeating the Orders to take to the Boats I was knock'd down by a stone and rising receiv'd a Stab with a *pahoa* in the shoulder, my Antagonist was just upon the point of seconding his blow when I shot him dead, the business was now a most miserable scene of confusion — the Shouts and Yells of the Indians far exceeded all the noise I ever came in the way of, these fellows instead of retiring upon being fir'd at as Captain Cook and I believe most People concluded they would, acted so very contrary a part, that they never gave the soldiers time to reload their Pieces but immediately broke in upon and would have kill'd every man of them had not the boats by a smart fire kept them a little off and pick'd up those who were not too much wounded to reach them. After being knock'd down I saw no more of Captain Cook, all my People I observ'd were totally vanquish'd and endeavouring to save their lives by getting to the Boats — I therefore scrambled as well as I could into the Water and made for the pinnace which I fortunately got hold of, but not before I receiv'd another blow from a stone just above the Temple which had not the pinnace been very near would have sent me to the Bottom."

Cook was dead. No eye witness on the shore saw how. Afterwards the account was put together. When Cook gave the order to fire, he turned and waved to the boats to come in to take them off. The signal was misunderstood by those on board as a cease-fire. The moment they stopped shooting the Hawaiians rushed in, knocked over Cook on the edge of the water, stabbed him with an iron spike and as he tried to get up, beat him to death with stones. They killed a total of six Englishmen and despite the fact that they were being shot at by both small arms in the boats and cannon from the *Resolution,* seized the bodies and carried them away. Throughout, only the third officer of the *Resolution,* John Williamson, who was in charge of the ship's launch refused to come in to assistance and threatened to shoot any of his crew if they attempted to do so, an action which has never been properly explained.

The English now had the unpleasant task of watching as the bodies of their comrades were carried off, being beaten with clubs.

Among the bitter recriminations afterwards, Cook himself came in for criticism. It was generally agreed that had he quit the shore immediately after deciding not to take Kalaniopuu hostage, he would have walked away unmolested. Instead he whiled away precious time as tension built up round him and the confidence of the Hawaiians grew.

The state of hostility continued for several days. The English were obliged to repair the main mast of the *Resolution.* They wanted to get back the bodies of their dead for a proper burial. There was also a desire for vengence. Captain Clerke was now in command of both ships and his immediate reaction was to warp the ships close to shore and lay down a cannonade to destroy the village and as many of its inhabitants as possible. He cooled his temper much to the discontent of both ship's crews and the cannons were not levelled in a devastating barrage. There were, however, additional provocations despite an attempt by the priests and the *ali'i* at reconciliation. On the 16th a piece of flesh was brought abroad. The priest who brought it said it was part of the late Captain Cook. The Hawaiians had taken out the bones as they would have in honouring their own chief and were preparing these for proper burial. The bones were in possession of Kalaniopuu.

On the 17th a man came to the foreshore and waved a hat at the ships. It was recognised as Cook's. The same man flung a stone towards the ships from a sling and directed a number of insults. In this he was supported by a large crowd. Clerke trained the cannon on them and fired several rounds which quickly dispersed the crowd. Among them was the same man of *fierce countenance*, the young prince Kamehameha, who was wounded. It was a lesson he was to remember well and one which would eventually make him the ruler of all the Hawaiian islands.

On the 20th, following the ratification of a firmer truce, more remains of Captain Cook were delivered to Clerke. In presenting the remains, the Hawaiians gave an account of their own loss in the battles. They had lost four *ali'i* (chiefs) and six others were wounded; 25 commoners were killed and 15 were wounded. On the 21st most of the bones of Cook were brought to the ship and later the two barrels of Cook's gun. On Monday the 22nd of February the remains of Captain James Cook were committed to the deep in accordance with English custom. On the 23rd the ships weighed anchor and sailed out.

KAMEHAMEHA THE KING

The king of the island of Hawaii, Kalaniopuu, designated his oldest son Kiwalao his successor and Kamehameha the keeper of the war god, Kukailimoku. The two step-brothers of Kiwalao, Keoua Kuahuula and Keoua Peeale, were to share in the re-distribution of lands, as was customary, following the death of Kalaniopuu. Kiwalao was unable to do this to everyone's satisfaction and a civil war broke out. Kiwalao was killed and a new struggle for succession developed between Keoua Kuahuula and Kamehameha, complicated by a continuing war between Kamehameha and Kahekili of Maui. A series of pitched battles were fought on the island of Hawaii between Kamehameha and Keoua during which Kamehameha was further harrassed by raids from Maui. And when he turned his attention to Maui and fought the successful battle near the Iao Needle (page 120-121), his plantations at Waimea and Kohala were devastated by Keoua.

The war between Kamehameha and Keoua lasted nine years. It allowed Kahekili time to put the islands of Lanai, Molokai and Oahu under his rule; Kauai was under the rule of his brother.

In 1790 after a desperate pitched battle which neither side could claim to its advantage, Kamehameha was given a prophecy which said that if he re-built the *heiau* at Puukohola at Kawaihae, near Waimea (see page 110), he would become the supreme ruler of the Island of Hawaii. The re-construction of the *heiau* co-incided with another incident, which was interpreted by Kamehameha as a favourable sign; half of the army of Keoua, marching through the Kilauea volcano area was killed when the wind changed and smothered them with poisonous gasses from a sudden eruption. The direction of the march of those who died can be seen to this day in the footprints trail in the Volcanoes National Park.

Kamehameha followed up with successful battles and eroded the following of Keoua to the point where he was unable to prosecute the war successfully. The *heiau* Puukohola was finished and awaited its consecration. Kamehameha sent envoys to Keoua asking him to end the war and arrange peace. The meeting which was arranged on the beach at Kawaihae was also a death sentence for Keoua and the chiefs who accompanied him. There are those who say that Kamehameha tricked his rival; others who say that Keoua knew he had lost, knew also that he and the chiefs with him, who came in that canoe, proud in their bright feather caps and cloaks, were about to die.

As he stepped ashore, a spear struck him in the chest. The armed men who surrounded the canoe quickly slaughtered the others. Their bodies were laid before Kukailimoku. The prophecy was fulfilled.

Kamehameha turned his attention to Kahekili in Maui. It was a war that the fierce Kamehameha pursued with vigour. His final success had to wait until Kahekili was dead and his kingdom equally divided between his son, Kalanikupule and his younger brother, Kaeo, and the chance intervention in the civil war between them by European ships. Kalanikupule won. He made a mistake in seizing the European ships, and loading them with his firearms for a projected invasion of the Island of Hawaii. The sailors in a counter-attack retook the ships and delivered the cargo of weapons to Kamehameha.

Kamehameha raised an army of 16,000 men; took Maui, Molokai and landed at Waikiki for his final battle with Kalanikupule. It was fought in the Nuuanu Valley with the Oahu force swept up by artillery and musket fire until finally in desperate hand-to-hand combat the survivors were forced over the steep cliffs at the end of the valley. Kalanikupule, unlike Keoua, escaped into the bush. Not for him the dignity of facing death among his vanquished warriors; he was hunted down and killed and his body was laid before Kukailimoku.

Only Kauai remained to be taken and eventually her young ruler, Kaumualii, acknowledged Kamehameha his king.

THE CORMORANTS ON THE BEACH

At the time when Kamehameha established his kingdom, the islands of the north and south Pacific were on the verge of European exploitation. There were features which made them attractive: sandalwood; sperm whales and land. The men at first attracted to exploit this area for their own advantage, were hard, ruthless adventurers. They were aptly described by a chief in Fiji: "... the cormorants who stalk upon the beach..." They brought with them guns, liquor and a overwhelming ambition to wrest away the power from the islanders. The missionaries for a time acted as a counter-balance, but in the end, it was an inevitable process. First the chiefs lost their power through the abandonment of the strict laws of their pagan gods; next, they were further corrupted by drink and debouchery and raked by debt. The merchants who had come a short while before with so little, now became the new princes. The Hawaiian was replaced with more compliant labourers; Chinese, Portugese, Filipino, Japanese and a new flood of *haoles* (whites) from America. It was, for those who had eyes to see, a requiem for a kingdom.

In 1893 the last Monarch of the dynasty founded by Kamehameha, the wilful Queen Liliuokalani, was deposed. Next year her supporters tried a coup which failed. It was used as a pretext to force Liliuokalani to sign her abdication and complete and unconditional renounciation of the throne. Four years later the islands became a territory of the United States and in 1959, a State of the Union.

HAWAII TODAY

The turbulent years of political anxiety have given way to a busy cosmopolitan population. Yankee ingenuity and Oriental husbandry, patience and hard work have made the islands a showplace. It has the world's most efficient sugar industry and the largest pineapple plantation, a boom économy and a tourist industry designed to cater for millions of mainlanders. It has the climate, the scenic grandeur and its own unique spirit of *aloha*. It is in fact, à unique spot in the world.

POINTS OF INTEREST

The State of Hawaii is composed of eight principal islands with a total land area of 6,421 square miles. The islands are (in order of size) Hawaii, 4,021 square miles; Maui 728; Oahu 602; Kauai 553; Molokai 259; Lanai 141; Niihau 72 and Kahoolawe 45. All the islands except Kahoolawe are inhabited. There are an additional 11 islets in the State but these have a total land area of only five square miles and none are inhabited.

The capital is Honolulu on the island of Oahu. Hilo on Hawaii is the next city of importance. Pearl Harbour in Honolulu was the scene of a surprise attack by 200 Japanese planes on December 7, 1941. The attack caused tremendous damage and loss of life but did not impair the United States to strike back. The entry of the United States into the war because of this attack, in the end not only sealed the fate of Japan, but also of Germany and Italy. A tour through the port takes you past the *U.S.S. Arizona,* which is now a national monument.

Geography: The islands are the tips of volcanic mountains rising steeply from the base of the ocean, which is extremely deep. Therefore, the highest mountain, Mauna Kea is extremely high at 13,796 feet above sea level. The islands were formed through volcanic eruptions of the mountains and volcanic activity still goes on in Hawaii. The twin peak next to Mauna Kea, Mauna Loa, is an active volcano linked to the Kilauea caldera, on its eastern side. Eruptions are frequent and give the countryside a devastated appearance. On the credit side, the flow of lava into the ocean is creating more land; on the debit ledger, it is destroying fertile land in its path. Though the cooled lava is itself fertile, it takes many years before it has broken down sufficiently for agricultural production. The eruptions are not violent and usually create a great deal of visitor interest. It is possible to walk up to the edge for a close view of the boiling lava and the hissing, crimson fountains which sometimes shoot up high into the sky. These displays are invariably most spectacular during the night.

Former eruptions which created the islands are also responsible for the visually dramatic countryside — the great *pali* (cliffs) found on all the islands; the tremendous crater on top of *Haleakala,* the 10,000 feet high mountain of Maui; the Iao Needle; Kalalau and Waimea canyons of Kauai; Kalaupapa of Molakai; the great water falls and the beautiful bays and coves and beaches.

Climate: Hawaii's famed climate combines with the reputation for scenery to make the State an ideal tourist resort. Winter and summer merge into one, the sun shines (except at Hilo?) but even where it rains a great deal, there are visual rewards. Waimea on Hawaii is a good example. The rain falls on fertile soil and the grass grows to feed excellent beef. But the important thing about Hawaii's climate is the fact that you can choose whatever suits you. There is a dry and wet side depending on whether you are on the windward or lee side of each island; warm at sea level regardless of season and cool enough up the mountains to enjoy a fire at night.

The people: Almost every nationality in the world may be found in Hawaii. The principal race is Caucasian with a large number of part Hawaiians, Japanese, Filipino, Chinese, Korean and Puerto Ricans. There are also Samoans, Portuguese, Negroes and Indians. The total population is now close to a million persons and tourists add another million each year. The overall impression of the various races in *aloha* shirts and the tourists in their distinctive bermudas and ankle-length sox, is both colourful and fascinating.

Opposite, famous Hawaiian flowers — the unique and rare
silversword and the anthurium

Waikiki, Honolulu.

New Year festival, Diamond Head crater, with Honolulu
beyond.

They fly in from the wintery cold of the Mid-West and
step out into the warmth of Hawaii to a greeting of flower
leis and get whisked off to cocktails at sunset in Waikiki.
The airline, American; the hotel, the Halekulani.

Overleaf — the yacht harbor, Waikiki with Diamond Head
in the background

Left to right, the Iolani Palace; statute of Kamehameha I;
band rotunda, Palace grounds; National Memorial Cemetary
of the Pacific, Punchbowl and (below) detail of Corinthian
iron columns, cast in San Francisco, for the palace; barracks.

Below, high-rise, Downtown Honolulu and Waikiki. Opposite,
hotel, Waikiki. Overleaf — north-west Oahu from Waialua
towards Kaena Point.

BYODO - IN
FIRM IN THE BELIEF THAT THE CULTURE AND RELIGIONS OF OUR ANCESTORS SHOULD BE PRESERVED, THE VALLEY OF THE TEMPLES CORPORATION HAS CONSTRUCTED THIS REPLICA OF JAPAN'S FAMED BYODO-IN.
AN ADVISORY COMMITTEE OF HAWAII'S BUDDHIST BISHOPS SELECTED BOTH THE TEMPLE AND ITS SITE. THE ADVISORS WERE REV. RYUE IKOMA, BISHOP RYUSHIN OKIHARA AND BISHOP KANJITSU IIJIMA OF NICHIREN MISSION OF HAWAII; BISHOP TETSUEI KATODA OF SHINGON MISSION OF HAWAII; BISHOP ZENKYO KOMAGATA OF SOTO MISSION OF HAWAII; BISHOP TENRAN MORI OF PALOLO HIGASHI HONGWANJI; BISHOP RYOICHI SHIRAYAMA
OF HIGASHI HONGWANJI MISSION OF HAWAII; BISHOP CHITOKU MORIKAWA, BISHOP SHOJITSU O'HARA, AND BISHOP KANMO IMAMURA OF HONPA HONGWANJI MISSION OF HAWAII; BISHOP SHINKO NAKASHIMA, BISHOP SHINGA INAGAKI, AND BISHOP KYODO FUJIHANA OF JODO MISSION OF HAWAII.
GROUNDBREAKING CEREMONIES WERE HELD ON JAN. 12, 1966. BYODO-IN WAS DEDICATED WITH PRIVATE BUDDHIST CEREMONIES ON JUNE 7, 1968, NEARLY 100 YEARS TO THE DAY THAT THE FIRST JAPANESE IMMIGRANTS ARRIVED IN THE HAWAIIAN ISLANDS. VALLEY OF THE TEMPLES HAS ERECTED THIS TEMPLE AS PART OF ITS SERVICE TO ALL RACES AND CREEDS.

Young lovers above the lookout at Nuuanu Pali, looking
back along the Nuuanu Valley. The forces of Kamehameha I
drove the army of Oahu up the valley forcing many to jump
to their death from the *pali*.

Sea Life Park, Makapuu, Paula "Lokelani" Look
rides the false killer whale and overleaf - - - she joins
her dolphins.

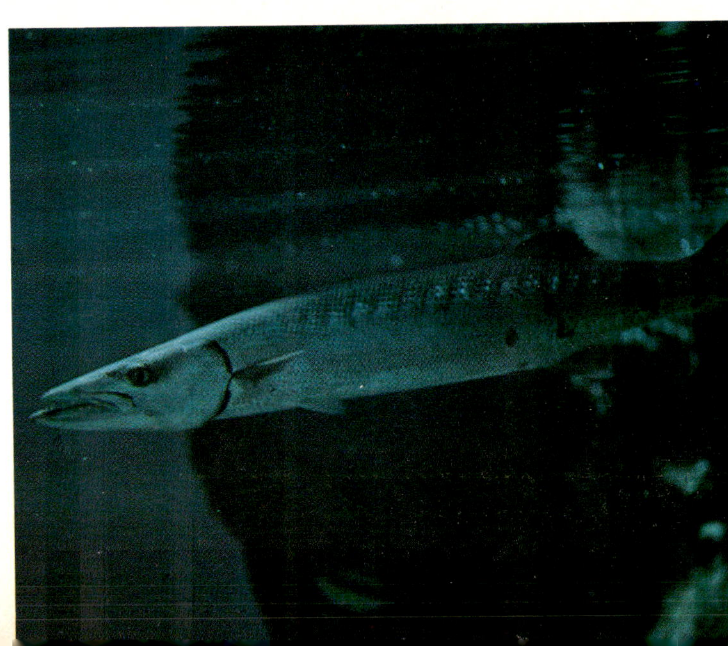

Polynesian Cultural Center, Laie, Oahu.

The kids show, Ala Moana Shopping Center, Honolulu.

The people: Hawaii must be the most cosmopolitan state in the world.

Faces, young and old. Overleaf — a young crab fisherman,
Molokai, and Hawaii's famous "suck-'em-up" Don Ho.

PALACE

It could only happen in Hawaii: a 12-year-old rides his motor-bike in backcountry Oahu. His father bought three motor bikes as a Christmas present — one each for his three boys. The 12-year-old is the oldest. Opposite, candid view, New Year festival, Diamond Head crater.

Hawaiian surf earned the respect of Captain James Cook
when he discovered the islands in 1778. It now commands
the respect of surfers from throughout the world. Below
body surfers Kealakekua Bay, where Cook was killed.
Opposite, big surf at Haena, Kauai.

Surfer and surfer's girl friend, Honolua Bay, Maui.

Candid view: from girl watching to looking at kimono-clad
Japanese at Waikiki.

Nick's
Fishmarket
WAIKIKI

Hawaiian women. What a marvellous blend. Right, Patrice
Wayne in the evening on the edge of the Kalalau lookout,
Kauai. Overleaf — nude, City of Refuge, Honaunau, Hawaii.

Two waitresses from Kauai and a stewardess, Hawaiian
Airlines.

The island of Kauai: Hawaii's most famous fish pond, the *Menehune* pond near Nawiliwili, Lihue. Center, Kauai Surf Hotel, Nawiliwili and, right, the famous Lumahai Beach near Hanalei. Overleaf — rice paddies and *taro* fields, Hanalei Valley.

Kalalau Valley, Kauai, in the evening. Opposite, storm
clouds, Anahola. Overleaf — Waimea Canyon and a cabin
in Kokee Park.

Young woman, Taylor's Camp, Haena, Kauai. Opposite,
fisherman at sunset near the Spouting Horn, Poipu.
Overleaf — start of the Na Pali Coast, northeast Kauai.

Hanalei, Kauai.

Eruption, 1972, Hawaii Volcanoes National Park.

Left, Waimea, Island of Hawaii; below, Painted Church, Kealakekua. Overleaf — Laupahoehoe Point, Hawaii.

Waipio Valley, Opposite, Hawaiian god figures, City of
Refuge, Honaunau. Overleaf — sunset, City of Refuge,
Honaunau.

Left, *paniolo* driving dairy herd, Naalehu. Below, bulls in contest, Parker Ranch, Waikii. Overleaf — Puukohola *heiau* built by Kamehameha in 1790-91 on the site of a former *heiau*, because of a prophecy that if he did so he would become the supreme ruler of the island of Hawaii. The prophecy became true when in 1791 the body of his chief rival, Keoua Kuahuula, was offered here as a sacrifice. Opposite, the ski slopes of Mauna Kea, nearly 14,000 feet high.

Left, Haleakala crater, Maui. Below former residence, now a school, Pukalani, Maui. Overleaf — left to right, cattle at Hana; view at Kipahulu; Lahaina views. Below left, whaler's museum, Kaanapali; Baldwin House; whaling ship; aerial of Maui Surf Hotel, Kaanapali.

1890
1970
GREAT EVENT
THE SUGAR CANE TRAIN
of The
Lahaina-Kaanapali
& Pacific
RAIL ROAD
MAUI, HAWAII
Travelers for Pleasure, Health or Business
Train leave the lusty old whaling town of
LAHAINA
KAANAPALI
VOYAGERS FROM AMERICA AND ALL OTHERS!
AUTHENTIC RECONSTRUCTED 1890 HAWAIIAN RAILROAD
PASS THROUGH MOUNTAINS AND ALONG SEASHORE
ONLY HAWAIIAN RAILROAD IN THE WORLD!
AKAHELE I KE KA'AAHI
Fares: $2.00 Roundtrip. Children $1.50. Babes in arms free.
INQUIRE ABOUT VALUABLE CANDY DANCER PASS
MAKAI CORPORATION
THIS POSTER FOR SALE
AT TICKET WINDOW

Hana Ranch, Maui.

Taro fields, Keanae.

The Iao Needle, Maui, top. Below, a rare view from the
side, approximately a third of the way up. As far as I know
I was the fifth person to climb to the top — the first one
with a camera. This must be a unique view. Overleaf — shore
break wave Keanae. Right, an avenue of pines, Napili, Maui.

Lanai-Molokai: below, young boys with a throw net,
Molokai. Right, Lanai, sunset view from Molokai.

Family fishing, Kawela, Molokai. Overleaf — foal and mother, Lanai; Catholic Church, Lanai City; Pineapple, Lanai; below left, falls, Halawa Valley, Molokai; abandoned church, Halawa Valley; petroglyphs, Lanai; sign at Lanai airport and, evening scene, Molokai;

LANAI
"The Pineapple Island"
WORLD'S LARGEST
PINEAPPLE PLANTATION
GROWER OF FAMOUS Dole PRODUCT

Kalaupapa lookout, Molokai.

Tree-fern and orchids, Hilo, Island of Hawaii.

JAPAN
Mariannas
Guam
Phillipines
Caroline Is
Marshall Is
Gilbert Is
New Guinea
Solomon Is
Ellice Is
New Hebrides
FIJI
New Caledonia
AUSTRALIA
NEW